Hamster Party

Written by Jeanne Willis

Illustrated by Emma Levey

OXFORD
UNIVERSITY PRESS

OXFORD
UNIVERSITY PRESS

Great Clarendon Street, Oxford, OX2 6DP, United Kingdom

Oxford University Press is a department of the University
of Oxford. It furthers the University's objective of excellence
in research, scholarship, and education by publishing
worldwide. Oxford is a registered trade mark of Oxford
University Press in the UK and in certain other countries

Concept © Jeanne Willis 2017
Illustrations © Emma Levey 2017
Inside cover notes written by Sam Keeley

British Library Cataloguing in Publication Data
Data available

ISBN: 978-0-19-841475-9

12

Paper used in the production of this book is a natural, recyclable product
made from wood grown in sustainable forests. The manufacturing process
conforms to the environmental regulations of the country of origin.

Printed in China by Shanghai Offset Printing Products Ltd

Acknowledgements

Series Editor: Nikki Gamble

The manufacturer's authorised representative in the EU for product
safety is Oxford University Press España S.A. of El Parque Empresarial
San Fernando de Henares, Avenida de Castilla, 2 – 28830 Madrid
(www.oup.es/en or product.safety@oup.com).OUP España S.A. also
acts as importer into Spain of products made by the manufacturer.